Each day, we write
about Show and Tell
in our journals.

3

On Monday, Emilia
brought a tiny goldfish
to Show and Tell.
It swam in its bowl.

4

On Tuesday, Amid
brought a green frog
to Show and Tell.
It hopped
on the teacher's leg.

5

On Wednesday, Lisa
brought a model glider
to Show and Tell.
It flew through the air.

6

On Thursday, Greg
brought a basketball
to Show and Tell.
It rolled out the door.

7

On Friday, I brought
my pet snake
to Show and Tell.
It wrapped
around my arm.
The class ran
down the hall!

8